Occupation Europe

1945–1946

As Witnessed by a 19-Year-Old GI

Lou Satz

Printing and design by

Falcon Books
San Ramon, California

ISBN: 978-0-9798855-0-1

Published by

Louis K. Satz and Associates

louksatz@comcast.net

PRINTED IN THE UNITED STATES OF AMERICA

Dedication

I am dedicating this book to two heroic World War II veterans who served their country with honor and courage.

Bob Tharratt, England 1943

Ray Slominski, England, 1942

Both of these men were in the 8th Air Force and both were ball turret gunners in B-17 bombers. Ray was in the 91st Bomb Group and was one of the first American airmen shot down over occupied Europe in WWII. He became a POW in December 1942 when his plane was shot down over France. Bob was in the 96th Bomb Group and became a POW in September 1944 when his bomber was shot down over Germany. Both men survived and went on to become leaders in their community.

Ray Slominski and Bob Tharratt, 2006

I am also dedicating this book to four young men very dear to me. I predict that these four young men will become leaders in a new generation.

Rory Satz, age 12

Robert Fishman, age 21

Jesse Sachs, age 18   Daniel Montalvo, age 17

As a grandfather or an uncle to these young men, I hope that they might develop an even greater appreciation of the importance of history and communication with diverse people from many different backgrounds.

I also hope that they will always support negotiation with maximum efforts and also consider warfare as a last means to resolve global disputes.

Acknowledgements

Many people have made major contributions that enabled me to write this book.

Jerry Whiting was indispensable with his great talent for researching and locating difficult facts. His experience in law enforcement enabled him to not only interview key people, but to articulate his findings in a concise and readily understood manner. Jerry also was tremendously helpful in the production of the book including scanning and formatting the photographs. He is an excellent editor as well as writer.

Bill Armstrong is a new friend who served 41 months in combat and in the Army of Occupation (Germany and Austria). He brought me a huge amount of material, particularly that of his exciting, sometimes dangerous, experiences.

Congresswoman Ellen Tauscher and her chief of staff in Walnut Creek, California, Karen Tedford, were totally committed to helping me verify my personal experience aboard the USS General Stuart Heintzelman, which I call "The Ship of Shame." They were tenacious, using all of the influence of their office in attempting to investigate my serious allegations of a "cover up" by a member of one of our naval or Merchant Marine fleet. Unfortunately, I now acknowledge that it is a closed issue. However, if anyone who reads this book could supply any substantiation of my allegations, I would deeply appreciate your contacting me.

I am very grateful to Bill Billet, founder and president of the United States Forces Austria Veterans Association (USFA) who has been generous in making pertinent information available to me. Recently I joined this organization of approximately 400 men who served in Austria between 1945 and 1954. They are a great bunch of patriotic men and women.

I met some of these veterans either by telephone, e-mail, or snail mail. These people were eager to exchange experiences as well as supply me with books, articles, photographs and suggestions. Among this group is John F. Bednarezyk, Clarksville, Indiana; John F. W. Koch, Evansville, Indiana; Bob Rogots, Las Vegas, Nevada; George Hooker, Frostproof, Florida, and Bob Hodges, St. Augustine, Florida. I also want to acknowledge four special people: Peter Finlayson, John Darling, Tom Conroy and Larry Green. These great pals suffered through dozens of Saturday morning breakfasts, tennis court matches, or Scrabble games where they (almost always) tolerated listening to my efforts in getting this book written and published. They may not even have to read the book. They've heard it all.

Thank you, Bev Fellows, who worked so well getting this manuscript ready for publication.

I could not write this book without giving a special acknowledgement to my commanding officer, Captain John Carley, for his leadership and the opportunities he gave me. He made my relatively brief but significant period in military service a meaningful experience.

From the time I bid Captain Carley goodbye in Linz, Austria until the time we again met in Monterey, California it was almost

35 years. Since that time John and Ulli, his lovely war bride, have met with members of my family on several occasions and while we do not see each other frequently, we still communicate.

Ruth Brophy provided me with personal memories of her activities as a teenager both during the war and the aftermath of hostilities.

Johannes Haas-Heye and his son Christoph contributed incisive observations of postwar events in both Germany and Austria, which greatly enhanced my personal observations.

And most important, thank you, Nancy. You tolerated the many hours of my absence while I was busy working in my study. And you continually demonstrated to me your great talents as an editor.

Thank you all!

About the Author

Lou with sons Jonathan (left) and Jay (right)

Born in Chicago, Lou Satz graduated from the University of Illinois after majoring in political science and marketing.

For 25 years, he served as senior vice president of sales and marketing for Bantam Books in New York City. He was also a consultant to Random House, Simon & Schuster, the World Book Encyclopedia and Passport Books, for which he was also the publisher.

He has traveled extensively and continues to consult for independent authors and publishers.

At present, Lou lives in Walnut Creek, California.

Contents

Prologue

I was 14 years old when Japan made its treacherous attack on Pearl Harbor on December 7, 1941. I remember saying to my dad, who served as a naval officer in World War I, "I'm too young to join the military services, but how can I help?"

My dad, knowing the magnitude of the conflict, said, "Son, it's going to be a long war and there will be difficult times for everybody. There will be plenty to do by everyone in this country."

The kids on the block learned how to identify enemy aircraft and assisted the air raid warden. All of us worked on small victory gardens and took part-time jobs so we could buy war bonds. Any person in service could hitch a ride to any place. And my dad, who never before had picked up a hitchhiker, always picked up anyone in uniform.

If we saw a blue star in the window of an apartment or house, or especially a gold star, we knew that a relative of that household either had a son, brother or husband in the service, or had lost a loved one. We would ring their bell and say, "Madame, is there anything I can do for you today?"

Studs Terkel wrote in his marvelous oral history "The Good War," "…it was truly a memorable part of our lives."

So, why am I writing this book? Because many decisions were made in this relatively short post-war period that affect the world today. And history of this period should be better understood by each of us.

Second, the rapidly diminishing number of men and women who served in WWII and immediately after are now dying at the rate of almost 1,500 a day. Their stories, and the lessons that can be learned from these experiences should continue to be passed on to the coming generations.

That brings up one additional reason for me to write this book and it's a totally personal one. I want my children and grandchildren by reading it to know how the experiences that I write about affected my personal growth.

Introduction

On the 3rd Thursday of every month, about 30 men, mostly veterans of WWII, meet for lunch in a private dining room of a Walnut Creek, California restaurant. This monthly lunch was started by two men, Bob Tharrall and Ray Slominski, who wanted to exchange their wartime experiences. Within a short time, this group grew to 50 members from virtually every branch of the military services who eagerly awaited the friendships and opportunities to reminisce. Some were eager to share experiences; others, for various personal reasons, had no desire to share war stories but simply wanted to be with those who shared this experience that we call WWII.

Three years ago, I joined this group as possibly the youngest member. I was probably one of the few men who had not seen combat, been shot at, been captured and/or been a prisoner of war, wounded or endangered in any way. It was a unique position to be in with these combat-savvy, war-weary, heroic guys, but I was in for a real surprise.

Jerry Whiting (left), Dan Cavalier (right) on the USS
Hornet, 2003

We sat around the lunch table, exchanging our feelings about
being in service. We spoke about the sacrifices required and the
patriotism that manifested itself because of the sacrifices made.
And for some reason, these guys liked the stories of *my* experience and interpretation of my own contribution to the post-war
occupation efforts. These included the Cold War with Russia, the
Holocaust survivors with their unbelievable experiences as well
as the beginning of the Marshall Plan that energized the world's
economy.

Soon five of us, Bob Tharratt (our leader), Hank O' Hagen,
Ray Slominski, Dan Cavalier, and I, embarked on a plan to publish a book, telling the personal stories of many members of this
group. We were joined by Jerry Whiting, the son of Sergeant

(L to R) Hank O'Hagen, Lou, Dan Cavalier, Bob Tharratt, Ray Slominski.
Walnut Creek, California, 2005

Wayne B. Whiting, tail gunner on a B 24 with the 485th bomb group, flying out of Venosa, Italy.

Jerry had written a biography of his father, *I'm Off to the War, Mother, But I'll Be Back*, and was busy finalizing his second book, *Don't Let the Blue Star Turn Gold*, a carefully researched book, telling the stories of many of the thousands of American airmen who were shot down during the air war over Europe.

Jerry became an indispensable member of our book publishing group. His 25 years as a tenacious fact-finding police officer made him invaluable in searching out fascinating data and writing with clarity and emotion. His book brought closure to the families and friends who had lost their loved ones in the air battles of WWII and never knew the facts of the capture or deaths of these brave men.

For a number of reasons, many members of our group were reluctant to tell their stories because of the painful experiences they had encountered and their inability to express their feelings. Unfortunately, our proposed book was never published. However, Neil Looker, a documentary film producer whose father also served in WWII, learned of the efforts to publish our book. He convinced five of us—Bob, Ray, Hank, Dan and me— that because of the diversity in our backgrounds, we'd have a lot to offer his documentary.

Jean and Ray Slominski, Walnut Creek, CA.

Consequently, in 2004, Neil produced "Lives Beyond the War." His film has been exhibited nationally in numerous film festivals and repeatedly screened on public television in our own community. All of us shared the experience of people on the street or in other public places asking, "Aren't you one of those WWII GIs on TV?"

Our dear friend Ray Slominski passed away in mid-2006. It was generally known that "The Little Giant," as our beloved Ray was called, was the inspiration for the role played by Steve McQueen in the film, "The Great Escape." All of us who knew Ray honor him for his great contribution to this country and his great friendships to all.

During the entire effort of our small group, both in working on our book concept, and the filming of "Lives Beyond the War," Jerry Whiting was indispensable.

My Story

In the spring of 1945, I was in my third semester at the University of Illinois in Urbana. As my 18th birthday was fast approaching as was the draft, I planned on going to Chicago to enlist in the Navy which I preferred over the army and one could enlist in the Navy at age 17.

It was an easy choice. The day I was scheduled to enlist was April 12th, the date of President Roosevelt's death. All public buildings were closed, so I cancelled my plans. That weekend, playing basketball, I was badly injured and my left leg, from hip to ankle, was enclosed in a full cast. By April 28th, my 18th birthday, I was registered at my draft board and a candidate for induction within the next few months.

In the summer of 1945, I was drafted into the U.S. Army, a sophomore student from Chicago. This was the same time as President Truman's decision to drop the atomic bomb on Hiroshima and Nagasaki, and Emperor Hirohito and his Minister of War, Hideki Togo, decided to surrender to the Allied Forces.

My army life began with 17 weeks of combat training, which included how to survive in the jungle, identify Japanese air craft, weapons and naval vessels and learn at least 50 idioms and key words in the Japanese language, supposedly helpful when we occupied Japan.

The 17-week training cycle was tough. I went in as a 135-pound kid and grew into a 175-pound powerhouse. At the training camp, I shared a hut with five other men. We got along fairly well. I became a hero to my platoon by being the star of the softball team. Because I was the only man with three semesters of college, I represented our platoon in the information and education weekly sessions. As a constant winner in these competitive activities, my platoon won the prize and being first in the chow line. What a way to gain respect!

While stationed at Camp Robinson, Arkansas, I had many opportunities to visit Little Rock on weekend passes. I was fortunate in having a very good friend who came from Little Rock while I was attending the University of Illinois. I became a frequent visitor to his parent's home and was treated like a member of the family, enjoying religious services, country club activities, meeting lovely young women and getting a warm feeling for a whole new community, much different from my Chicago environment.

One day while taking a public bus, I was sitting comfortably in the front end of the bus when a young African American soldier stepped into the seat next to me, smiled and said "Hello."

The next moment, two teenaged white boys grabbed the soldier, and using four letter words and threats, threw him off the bus onto the pavement. As I jumped up to help him, heavy hands grabbed me from behind, and a middle aged white man snarled, "Keep your seat, mister. This is what we do to people who break the law. If you interfere, you'll get the same treatment."

When I mentioned this incident to my hosts, they merely said, "We don't like what you saw, but this is what happens to black soldiers from the north who aren't advised by the army what they can expect down south."

I experienced anti-Semitism during basic training. I had pulled KP duty and my bunkmate of four weeks, Herbert Miller, was appointed an assistant to the company cook. I reported to Miller at 6:30 a.m. and greeted him. "Hey Herb, here I am." The words that came out of Miller's mouth were shocking. "You lousy Jew bastard! Before this day is over, I'll have you crawling in the dirt. You're going to clean every grease trap in this kitchen. You're going to make them shine—you rotten Christ killer!"

For the next eight hours, I cleaned out every grease trap in the company kitchen. It was a nightmare. I could hardly breathe. Twice I passed out and throughout the day I vomited. When I returned to my bunk, close to four o'clock that afternoon, my four bunkmates looked at me in disbelief. Miller had a cruel smirk on his face.

When the same situation occurred three weeks later, another bunkmate, Frank Stanky, offered to get back at Miller. I thanked him but said I would handle it myself. Everyone in the company despised Miller. Unfortunately, I had to experience a third and similar KP assignment with Miller before the training cycle was over.

Basic Training

Physical fitness and learning about the weaponry of combat, were our principal activities. Germany had surrendered in June; Japan surrendered in September, and for our 17-week basic training, virtually no changes were made in our instruction.

I was in a heavy weapons training company. All of us had to master every detail of our MI Gerand rifle, which was our basic weapon.

Training at Camp Robinson, summer 1945

In heavy weapons, we became experts in the operations of 50-caliber heavy machine guns, and 81-millimeter mortars, which operated as a four-man crew. Training on these weapons was virtually useless considering what our occupation responsibilities would necessitate in both Europe and Japan.

The physical training was great. In spite of the aches, pains and utter exhaustion, we became very tough and somewhat resourceful in knowing when and how to goof off. Besides the obstacle course and hand-to-hand combat training, six-man teams tossed eight-foot tree trunks about eight inches in diameter at each other. Although it was fun, there were a few broken bones as a consequence.

During a 10-minute break, I learned how to consume a Hershey bar, an orange and take a five-minute nap. I also gained almost 40 pounds during the training period.

Change of Plan

I was prepared to go to Japan and upon receiving my orders after basic training, lo and behold, those orders had me going to the occupation of Europe. I was thrilled. I didn't like the idea of meeting snakes, spiders and the possibility of malaria in Japan.

Immediately after my training cycle was over and I had returned from a 10-day furlough to Chicago, the Army offered the opportunity to thousands of recently trained troops to re-enlist in the regular army for one year. We would be promoted to private first class, and receive a 30-day furlough to begin the new one-year enlistment. I grabbed the opportunity as it gave me a specific discharge date that coincided with the beginning semester at the University of Illinois for the spring of 1947.

As it turned out, this decision worked completely to my advantage as some of my friends who had gambled on their discharge date remained in service for two to three months longer than I did. I was also asked if I wished to attend officer's training school and be stationed in Europe to become part of the post office division of the U.S. Army. This was a "no brainer" decision. It meant an enlistment of three years. That's why I eagerly accepted the one-year re-enlistment.

On My Way

I can't describe the feeling in my stomach as I boarded the ship and left the United States to join the army of occupation in Europe. Thousands of men were processed every week through various regional staging areas. Conditions were dismal and the

Army of occupation, Linz, Austria

men were apprehensive—long waits, lousy food, dismal barracks and a dreaded sense of "what's next?"

Aboard the ship, our sleeping quarters were four high, a strip of canvas and just about enough space to breathe. The odors were terrible, particularly when seasickness affected a good many of the troops. The war in Europe had been over for six months and Japan had surrendered a few months earlier. We all knew that there was no real danger, but we were none-the-less frightened and already very lonesome. None of my buddies of the last four months were with me and finding common interests with new men was difficult. The trip seemed endless but actually it took only about eight or nine days.

We arrived at Le Havre, France and after three days in Camp Philip Morris, we were placed in box cars on transport trains headed for Germany. Each car held about 40 men. We slept on the floor and ate lousy K rations.

On February 1, 1946, I arrived in Ebelsburg, Austria to join the 5th Infantry Regiment. By this time most of the combat soldiers were gone and our company was made up of 18-year-old immature guys, some interested in sex and minor black market activities with little knowledge of why they were there.

The Big Picture

Austria was at first classified as a conquered country, occupied by the four allied nations of France, Great Britain, Russia and the United States. Its designation later was classified as a liberated country. The priorities of what must be addressed were clearly defined and then executed by armies that had been trained for combat and various police activities such as guarding roadblocks, trains, bridges, interpreting, vehicle drivers, clerks and general administrative responsibilities.

Fortunately, careful postwar planning had been started in London months before the European invasion began because of the foresight of the allied commanders under the command of General Eisenhower. For some, it was difficult to see the entire big picture, particularly of a country like Austria that was not self-sustaining.

Over hundreds of years at least 12 different countries had conquered and occupied Austria. Now slave laborers, refugees, and soldiers from most European countries had, or would be living in this territory.

At the end of the war, over 10 million displaced persons (DPs) were living in Europe. There were 400,000 DPs in Austria, and over 120 DP camps in the American zone. There were huge logistical problems, but clearly stated and successfully addressed by our military commanders.

Following are some of the most important issues that had to be resolved:

- Self-government be created.
- How to handle the prisoners of war
- How to stabilize and maintain border security
- Create public health and welfare programs
- How to manage the logistics and care of the displaced persons
- Create the civil and military court systems
- Organize the distribution of the fuel supply for both the civilian and military requirements
- How to manage the transportation systems
- Restructure the public school system
- How to create and encourage the entire cultural (art, music, literature) programs

These issues and others had to be explored and then managed by our military forces, and to their credit, they accomplished many or most of these issues in a very efficient manner.

Assignments in Linz and Ebelsburg

Our principal duties were to inspect any individuals who looked suspicious passing from the Russian zone to our zone. There were four bridges between the American and Russian zones. Every week I met my Russian counterpart halfway on the bridge. He would give me an American $20 bill for a carton of cigarettes for which I had paid 50 cents. By the time I returned to the states, I had sent home over $1,700, which included my base pay of about $65 a month.

A few days after I arrived at Ebelsburg, two experiences really startled me. While I was in formation, a corporal who seemed to be in a state of either shock or drunkenness, staggered past our platoon and tried to line up with the third squad. The first sergeant, seeing him, swiftly walked over to the corporal and speaking kindly, motioned him gently towards the barracks. When I saw his face, it was frightening. His eyes were glazed and looking straight ahead. His face showed terror, which looked almost like a death mask, and his lips were trembling out of control.

I was a member of the third squad, and later that day I asked our sergeant what was wrong with the soldier. "Oh, Corporal Shields was in the lead company that liberated Dachau," replied the sergeant. "When he saw the ovens and the walking dead of the inmates, he jumped on a tank with a mounted 50 caliber machine gun. There were six German PWs standing nearby and screaming with rage. Shields opened up and killed all of them."

Linz/Urfahr Bridge, facing the Russian zone, 1946

The following day while I was on guard duty on the Danube River bridge between the American and Russian zones, I heard screaming and yelling coming from the Russians guarding their check point. Three men in a small rowboat, all civilians, were trying desperately to steer their boat under the bridge in order to escape to the American zone. The current kept pushing their boat into the open river. When the Russians sighted the exposed boat, they opened fire and almost immediately the Danube carried three dead men down river. These two events immediately made me aware of the reality of our mission. I took it very seriously for the rest of my entire tour of duty.

My experience on the bridge that day was the forerunner of the very negative opinion and apprehension I cultivated for our Russian allies. It's true that Russian soldiers and certainly millions of innocent civilians were killed, raped, tortured and brutally imprisoned by the German military machine. Perhaps the soldiers simply had no compassion for anyone who was not Russian. Civilians, who were unfortunate to live in those areas controlled by the Russian army, rarely saw or felt a moment of friendship, tolerance or help in rebuilding not only their lives but the basic structure of the cities and villages destroyed by the ravages of war. Many of the enlisted men were totally out of control with drunkenness and attacked innocent women who wanted no part of their sexual advances.

Fear manifested itself in almost every aspect of their lives and the Russian authorities did very little to control their underlings. Actually, some of our own troops were not such good examples of acceptable behavior. Basically, though, we made monumental efforts to feed, clothe, house people, reunite them with their families and help rebuild housing, schools, hospitals, roads and the entire infrastructure of their country.

I know of several soldiers who for personal reasons chose to stay in occupied Europe and assume a civilian life. They told me that they never went out without a loaded firearm in their belt. They made certain that their personal papers were up to date, because the consequences could be very serious for even minor infractions of the very strict rules the Russians created and implemented.

The American troops were for the most part helpful, especially kind to children, and I might say, very pleasant to young women, some of who eagerly cultivated warm friendships with our troops.

About five weeks into my stay in Ebelsburg, our company was down to about 160 men and we were all doing double duty. We had little time to sleep and were all exhausted. I hated this duty and became determined to find another assignment. One day our acting company commander posted a job notice on the bulletin board. "Seeking a typist to record the proceedings of Special Court Martials." I was desperate and convinced the lieutenant that I was the man for the job. I learned to type in one day, and I'm sure that this proactive effort of mine completely changed my army career.

When the assignment was over four weeks later, in appreciation, the lieutenant appointed me reconnaissance sergeant. I then worked on intelligence matters, black market activities, and was also placed in charge of a 60-man platoon.

Daily living outside military responsibilities were most unusual. First of all, because of food rationing, we couldn't go to a restaurant or coffee shop. Food there wasn't available. Everything was rationed and if you wanted to eat anything, it was either at your military base, PX or Red Cross center. Local currency meant nothing. Cigarettes were the most important medium of exchange, followed by chocolate, soap and gifts from the PX. Cigarettes would get your laundry done, get a shave, haircut and shoe shine, let you board the bus or trolley, sole your shoes, get your clothes dry cleaned, or support a full-time girlfriend. Feature films were changed twice a week and admission was free to the GIs.

The Information and Education Division had a tough job. They had to set standards and rules of behavior for unsophisticated young men, many of whom had never left their home towns before entering military service. The I&E also provided entertainment and travel opportunities for the troops.

The troop members either spent their recreational hours at the Red Cross or at local drinking establishments. The Red Cross staff was terrific, not only the professional women but the young, attractive local women who were very carefully selected and required to maintain a high degree of personal standards of behavior.

The Red Cross center in Linz was outstanding in every respect. It supplied ice cream, sandwiches, table tennis, telephone service to home, dancing, and quiet places to read, write letters and listen to music. The professional staff members were also good listeners for guys who wanted to talk about their own personal situations. When pulling guard duty along the Russian-American check points, nothing was more gratifying to the men than when a Red Cross jeep pulled up with hot coffee, cocoa and donuts, served by a cheerful, attractive Red Cross woman.

The entertainment programs were sometimes a different story. I remember once when a talented group of young USO actors drove many miles to perform a single performance of a current Broadway hit. I arrived with a buddy for an 8 p.m. performance. When we arrived 10 minutes before the scheduled time, we thought that we had come on the wrong evening. The theater was absolutely empty. One minute before curtain time, a WAC captain sat down near us.

The curtain came up and the setting showed a very beautiful Broadway actress' New York apartment. There were nine people on the stage. When the cast saw only the three of us in the audience, one actor stepped forward and said, "Thank you for coming. You expected to see a Broadway play. Well, you will, right now. Will you three theater fans please come up on the stage and sit on the big sofa. You're going to be total participants in this play and you will never forget it. Now please join us on the stage."

When the play was over (and it was hilarious), the nine performers and the three of us returned to the Red Cross for ice cream sodas. No, I never will forget that evening in the theater.

A friend from I&E scheduled a trip for me for two days and nights at the Pitter Hotel in Salzburg, a relatively short train ride from Linz.

The first weekend radically changed my whole new after-duty life. The American-operated Pitter Hotel was charming, a five-minute walk from the railroad station. It offered excellent food and a young pianist, Franz, to whom I gave a pack of cigarettes every Friday evening. He played both classical and popular music. Franz also arranged free tickets for me to attend the Salzburg Music Festival, which in 1946 reopened the for the first time in many years.

During the days, I strolled Salzburg, a beautiful city. I made side trips into the Bavarian Alps, and became greatly aware of Mozart and his music. Also during these visits, I conscientiously continued my efforts to visit the Glasenbach Displaced Persons Camp and to do whatever I could to assist the Holocaust survivors and their families. My visits to Salzburg afforded me many eventful days.

Return to Linz

In Linz, I could see men in business suits carrying brief cases. They would follow a horse and wagon, and gather the waste for fertilizer or as an add on for their homemade tobacco.

Women were easily available to the men who wanted female companionship. The venereal disease rate in our area sometimes reached 15 to 20 percent of a unit's personnel. Almost an epidemic.

One day the company got a new commander. He was a West Point graduate, a brilliant officer, and a fine athlete. His name was Captain John W. Carley. He was 22 years old and he changed my life.

Captain John W. Carley, Lou's commanding officer, 1946

Lou promoted to sargeant

Captain Carley quickly promoted me to sergeant. He was often given special assignments from the commanding general, and he relied on me to carry out some of these assignments. My world really opened up. Not bad for an 18-year-old kid. One of my assignments was working with survivors of the Holocaust (mostly, but not all Jewish). It was indeed a profound experience.

Later, while stationed in Ebelsburg, I served as a leader of a 60-man platoon. I was also the ranking intelligence non-commissioned officer in the battalion. One day I noticed a transport truck bringing in replacements. I recognized one of the replacements and asked the First Sergeant to assign this man to my platoon. The soldier was Herb Miller, the guy who made me clean out the grease traps back in Arkansas. No words or looks were exchanged between Miller and me for two days. Finally we had a conversation:

Miller: Sergeant, I got to talk to you.

Me: Talk!

Miller: I need privacy to talk.

Me: If you want to talk to me, talk!

Miller: OK, OK. Do you know who I am?

Me: You bet I do!

Miller: What are you going to do to me? I can't stand it any longer. I'm going crazy. How are you going to get back at me?

Me: Miller, you are a rotten piece of shit but if you think for one second, I am going to stoop to your level, you are badly mistaken. Now get lost.

I learned from this incident that I was capable, under the worst of circumstances, of taking the high road.

There were two types of soldiers in the Army at that time. First, there were still some combat veterans who were essentially non-commissioned and junior grade officers. I found these men competent, serious and if they were not regular Army, anxious to complete their service and return to their private lives.

Second were the men under 20 who came from all parts of the country and from every ethnic background. Of these men, some

Major General "Hollywood Harry" Collins

were relatively undisciplined, heavy drinking, sexually very active, and involved in minor black market activities.

One day General Collins made a surprise inspection of our company. We stood in company formation, and I was standing with General Collins and our first sergeant as we went up and down the ranks. The general was impressed as to how sharp our bloused trousers were relative to our combat boots. He asked one of our guys how he did it. The soldier said, "Sir, do you really want to know?"

The general howled with laughter as he saw each boot with a stretched condom blousing the pants leg. He turned to our First Sergeant and said, "From now on, no man goes off the base with less than three condoms. I trust they will know how to use the extra one!"

My work was interesting and eclectic. I investigated criminal and black market activities, among other things. One day on patrol with my driver, Pete Peterson from Chicago, we were on a country road and saw a small band of gypsies from Yugoslavia living in a makeshift camp. There was a young woman whom we recognized as a former girlfriend of our supply sergeant.

When we walked over and looked into her tent, we were surprised to see army blankets, uniforms and kitchenware. These people were obviously black marketers who lived off stolen army supplies. The next few minutes were terrifying. Pete moved towards our jeep as five or six men started to surround me—one armed with an ax handle, another a pitchfork, and another with an old rifle. I drew my unloaded 45 automatic and my assailants retreated. I dashed to the jeep and Pete and I took off. Ten minutes later we returned with six MPs, just as the gypsies, who had broken camp, were leaving.

There had been about 15 men and one woman in the gang. Traveling by horse and cart and living in small tents, they were a menace to both the military and civilian population. Two of the ringleaders and the woman were tried and convicted of larceny for stealing military material. I don't remember what their sentences were but in all probability a very short one since crime in Austria was pervasive and this was really a minor case.

Pete and I served as witnesses at the trial, and at this point it struck me that having the gypsy group of men surrounding me at their camp was one of the scariest events of my Army career.

Many days, Pete and I would leave our headquarters and travel within a radius of 20 to 30 kilometers, essentially along the Russian-American Danube River crossings. The American military had four checkpoints, including a rail crossing between Linz and Urfahr, where in my earlier days I had witnessed the murder by the Russians of three men who were attempting to cross into our zone. Guarding these checkpoints was one of the responsibilities of our unit.

Our random driving gave us the opportunity to see the countryside, drink warm beer (I never did get used to warm beer), while looking into black market possibilities, local accidents and on more than one occasion, investigate rumors that came from local sources. For example, we were told four Russian tanks were moving near the river with a 15-man patrol accompanying them. The truth was that three wagons with six men in a wagon were moving to harvest a crop. We almost never knew what we were looking for, but were prepared for almost any situation we'd encounter.

One morning when we were in formation, readying ourselves for the day's assignments, we heard an explosion and screams of agony. I was facing my platoon, looking towards our quarters, and I saw smoke and flames shooting out of the windows of our basement mess hall. Without thinking of the consequences, I rushed into the doorway of the basement and seconds later staggered out of the building, crying and throwing up. I had found three naked American soldiers and several displaced persons, who worked for us, standing there horribly burned and in shock. I cannot describe what they looked like. It was a nightmare!

While being cleaned, one of the stoves exploded for an unaccountable reason. That day, three of the victims died and the three other men survived with multiple burns over half of their bodies. Ironically, the new kitchen was moved to the top floor of our quarters and only a few months later, there was another explosion. It blew off the roof of our kitchen. Fortunately, the explosion occurred in the early morning and there were no injuries.

Train To Nowhere

On one assignment, I was responsible for a train headed for Germany carrying 800 slave laborers returning to their homes, and 40 German prisoners of war. We traveled almost five days on a single track. I had a team of four men who shared a boxcar containing canvas beds, a stove, a portable latrine and plenty of food and water. The other cars each held 30 to 40 people and whatever belongings they possessed.

One evening, when the train was stopped, I got off to observe the cars at the front. Suddenly the train started up. I was about 20 feet from the train and as it gained speed, I started running. I couldn't find a place to jump on when two pairs of very strong arms belonging to German PWs grabbed me and pulled me into the boxcar that held the other PWs. Out of breath and frightened, I thought I was in trouble. Not so. An English-speaking sergeant assured me that I was fine and in good hands.

I gave the PWs the two packs of cigarettes that I carried. The men told me that soon we all would be allies fighting the Russians, who were trying to take over the world. I stayed with these guys for over six hours, talking most of the night. Quite an experience.

One night, two days later, we were again sitting on a siding, waiting our turn on the one available track. As I was inspecting the train, a voice speaking English in a distinct southern accent said, "Good evening, sergeant, would you please give me a cigarette?" The woman, in her early 20s, dressed in jodhpurs, riding boots, a Western shirt complete with a bolo tie, was standing in the shadows. "My name is Trudi Muller, from Dresden, Germany, by way of Waco, Texas. Could we talk?" Trudi was either a great actress or the most authentic looking Texan one could imagine. Her story was as follows:

Her mother and father from Dresden were active supporters of Hitler's Third Reich. Trudi was born in Dresden in 1926 and immigrated to Texas in 1931. She was a typical Texan, loved popular music, was a member of the gymnastic club, a cheerleader and very popular in her early high school days.

She and her parents returned to Germany to serve the Third Reich. Her father was a captain in the Wehrmacht and at age 18, Trudi married an SS officer. Within the next few years, her mother was killed in the Dresden firebombing and her husband and father were killed while serving on the Russian front.

Trudi considered herself a woman without a country. She was convinced she had absolutely no future unless she married an American soldier, became a war bride and returned to America. She asked me if I would consider the two of us returning to Linz to apply for a marriage license. I was astonished and saddened with her story and request. I never saw her again.

The fact was that thousands of German/Austrian women, each with their own particular situation grabbed the opportunity to marry American G.I's. It was a thorough and tough procedure that they had to endure. First, they had to pass strict standards with the Chaplain Corps. Then they had to pass a tough Denazification Board. I knew of several friends who attempted this process and some of the marriages worked out extremely well, while others if not turned down, were total disasters after coming to the U.S. for their new life.

The Maverick Warrior

I n December 2006, I attended the monthly veterans lunch and was asked by Bob Tharratt, our group leader, if I would bring the fellows up to date on this book project, which had been discussed over the past year. After a few minutes one of our

Bill Armstrong, Vienna 1946

Vera Ivanovna Massuda, Vienna 1946

guests raised his hand and asked if I would answer a question. "Of course," I responded.

The inquirer introduced himself as Bill Armstrong. He asked: "Did you play ping pong at the Red Cross in Linz, Austria in January 1946?" I was astounded, and replied, "Yes, I did!" Many of the men sitting at our table howled with surprise and laughter as Bill and I hugged each other with total joy. Unbelievable! This was the beginning of a great new friendship.

Later when Bill and I went over this miraculous coincidence, we discovered that while we both did play ping pong at the Linz Red Cross in January 1946, we could not have played together as Bill left Linz for Vienna in mid-January of that year and I didn't arrive in Linz until the end of January. We did, however, solve the mystery. Bill had seen me several times when our documentary film "Lives Beyond the War" was televised on our local station. When he heard me talk about serving in Linz, he simply visualized the voice (and face) and made his discovery, which is totally understandable.

During the past few months, Bill, Jerry and I have formed a great new friendship. They have been of considerable assistance to me in researching and advising me on this book.

While Bill and I did share many similar experiences in Austria and Germany during the entire year of 1946, I thought it would be of interest to my readers if they could read Bill's remarkable story as he started out as an under-aged kid in the California reserves, and ended up in combat for over 200 days.

The following paragraphs are taken from a letter that Bill wrote to a long-lost buddy, Don Newlin, a wartime friend with whom Bill reconnected in 1996. These few paragraphs put into perspective Bill's eloquent and passionate emotions of his combat experiences.

I am a veteran of World War II like so many of us still alive who think back to those days with a degree of fondness. To the young folks of today, that war is ancient history, if they have any knowledge of it at all. Often I'm asked if I am referring to the Korean War. "No," I reply. "The war before that one." And they look puzzled. To me, that period was the greatest adventure of my life and not so long ago, as I remember it.

I can still see the faces of many of my buddies and hear their voices. The sounds of artillery still echo in my ears. And the smells…lordy, the smells! Burned towns and cities, rotting cattle, carcasses bloated with stiffly raised legs, dotting the fields from Normandy onward. The singular putrid odor of decaying human bodies, soldiers and civilians alike, is one that can never be confused with anything else. These are all part of the memories of war.

Yet, with all the bad things that happened, I have to admit that those were the most exciting, frightening, memorable days of my life, not counting the day I got married or the birth of my children. That's another subject entirely. Once in combat, it was so far removed from everyday normal living that there is nothing to compare to it. Like science fiction, in a way.

Before I go into Bill's occupation duty in Austria until his return to the United States in 1947, I'm including a paragraph taken directly from Bill's memoirs, relative to his combat activities, which started on Utah Beach, Normandy on September 7, 1944 and ended May 9, 1945. Their division, the 26th Yankee Division, was the last division to cease combat.

The Division had joined General Patton's Third Army on October 20, 1944. Combat took them through France, into Luxembourg and the Battle of the Bulge, across the Rhine into Germany, finally standing down from battles in Czechoslovakia, ending 210 days "on the line." He returned to Germany, then Austria, first stationed in Upper Austria, then transferred to Vienna in January 1946.

After reading Bill's memoir and the series of letters he wrote to his wartime buddy, Don Newlin, I got a sense of what this guy was all about. However, now knowing him personally, I have a real sense of who he is and how he was able to not only cope with unbelievable adversity but to thrive, survive and instill confidence and devotion to so many people in wartime and in his later life as well.

He was a maverick —a wise guy—very capable of doing funny stunts and getting away with them, even after getting caught. He lost his stripes a number of times. He found "unacceptable" ways to get the job done and also frequently squirmed his way out of trouble.

His values are honorable. He suffered a terribly painful injury in a non-combat incident and was told to accept a Purple Heart because of his injury. He turned it down because he felt he didn't earn it as did some of his seriously wounded buddies. This award would give him five points on his record and allow him an earlier trip home for discharge. Bill told me that if he had had that earlier discharge, he would not have met Vera, his loving war bride of 62 years.

Bill acknowledges how lucky he has been.

In August of 1945, the 263rd Field Artillery Battalion was quartered in Ranshoffen, upper Austria. It was on a local volleyball court that Bill met Vera Ivanovna Massuta. For Bill, it was love at first sight.

Vera was a displaced person whose home was the Ukraine. She was not only beautiful but an outstanding volleyball player, and nationally known throughout Russia as a world champion track and field star. She had been selected, trained and subsidized by the Russian government that highly valued her importance, and subsequently demanded that she be returned to Russia to fulfill her obligation to her country.

By October 1945, Vera and Bill were convinced that they wanted to share their lives together and Vera (with a lot of persistence and luck) avoided any possibility of being returned to Russia, while Bill returned to Vienna when he learned he could take his discharge there and be hired as a civil servant. By mid-January, he accomplished this, and was put in charge of a major motor pool. He went back to Ranshofen to pick up Vera and return to Vienna to start their new life.

Their trip from Linz to Vienna was a nightmare. The Russian guards at the train station and on the train itself, as well as when they were entering Vienna were a constant threat to the couple. At the worst possible moment of almost-capture (they had no official documents), Vera pleaded with Bill to shoot her (Bill was never without a loaded firearm) in case the Russians discovered her. Luck was with them and on January 26, 1946 they arrived in Vienna to begin their new life. They still were not married.

Bill became a civilian after 11 months of soldiering, yet he resided and ate in officer's quarters; Vera lived close by with friends.

Bill ultimately found a suitable apartment in Vienna and at last he and Vera were living together. They married in July of 1946 at Votivkirche, a magnificent gothic church. In November of that year, Thomas Church Armstrong was born.

When Vera, Bill and Thomas left Vienna, they had another frightening experience that threatened their safety while traveling through the Russian zone. It seemed that destiny was going to prevent them from assuming a normal, safe life in the United States. Again their luck prevailed.

Vera and Bill now reside in a beautiful Bavarian-type chalet in Walnut Creek, California. Their home has a spectacular view of a

Vera Ivanovna Massuda, Vienna 1945

nearby mountain range. Their house is filled with treasures they have accumulated in their lifetime of travel.

They have a daughter and two grandchildren, Julie Helene and Gregory Thomas. Unfortunately, Thomas passed away at the age of 36.

A Young Woman's Odyssey

When I thought my book was nearly complete and I was preparing for the publishing process, Nancy received an assignment from the *Rossmoor News* to interview and write about Ruth Brophy, a well-known local artist.

I learned from Nancy that Ruth was born and raised in Linz, Austria, where I spent nearly all of my overseas duty in the Army of Occupation immediately after World War II. Nancy arranged for me to meet Ruth so I could get a first-hand account of what it was like to be a civilian in the city of Linz and surrounding area in which I served. Ruth agreed to meet with me and we had several fascinating conversations. I'm pleased to record some of her experiences and observations as a young teenager in those difficult times.

Ruth lived with her parents and two sisters in what was an historical landmark hotel on the shore of the Danube River near the center of the city. The building had been a monastery, and it was constructed around about 1660. The structure was converted to an inn, catering to distant travelers. In the 1920s, Ruth's

Ruth Brophy as a young teenager in Linz

grandfather, a builder from Vienna, took over as owner and manager of the inn, which was family operated for many years.

Ruth has many memories of the heavy bombings by the Allied Forces, bombings which were aimed primarily at what was then the Herman Goring steel mills, one of Hitler's primary manufacturers of military weapons. In addition, the rail center was virtually wiped out by the British and American air forces. Ruth and her family spent many hours in the air raid shelters.

Hunger was an ongoing problem in the area. But after Ruth's father was drafted into the German Army, he was able to supply food for his family. When he became the driver of the commanding colonel of the area, the colonel and Ruth's father would drive out to the countryside and barter and sometimes "relieve" the farmers of food. Thus, the family rarely experienced hunger problems.

Ruth remembers that immediately after the end of the war, the hotel became the headquarters of the Criminal Investigation Corps (CIC) of the U.S. Army. Ironically, these headquarters

City of Linz, Austria, 1946

received weekly intelligence reports that my regiment created, but we never personally met with any personnel from the CIC. In addition, I now realize that the CIC headquarters was about 100 feet from the guard post that my regiment (and I) had maintained at the Linz-Urfahr Bridge over the Danube that separated the American and Russian zones.

Ruth gave me the background of the "05." The "05" represented the symbol of the Austrian resistance movement during the war years when the German army occupied Austria. The "05" connected Austrians of different religious, political beliefs, racial and ethnic backgrounds and occupations, all of whom struggled against the Third Reich.

Following the annexation of Austria by Germany in 1938 (the Anschluss) until the end of the war, 2,700 Austrians were executed for resistance activities. Sixteen thousand Austrian resistance fighters were murdered in concentration camps; 9,000 were executed in Gestapo prisons, and 65,000 Jews were murdered in ghettos and camps. In addition, 130,000 Austrians fled the country because of their religious, ethnic or racial backgrounds.

Ruth As a Witness

Again, ironically, Ruth's family hotel was one of the principal meeting places for some of the "05" activities and Ruth's father was an active participant.

I didn't know anything about this resistance movement until several months ago when I met Ruth. She told me that the bomb shelter where they spent hundreds of hours actually was located in an isolated section of the hotel where she and her family lived. The bottom foundation was underground and connected to the main building.

The British Air Force usually bombed during the night; the American Air Force, essentially based in Africa and Southern Italy, sent their bombers out in daylight. Sirens were sounded soon after the flight plans of the bombers were radioed to the Austrian targets, which allowed the civilians to reach the bomb shelter in ample time. Ruth and her family rarely sought refuge in the public shelter.

During the war and well into the days of American occupation, virtually no clothing was manufactured for the civilian population. Also, books were not published; cosmetics and film were unavailable and the public schools were not in full operation for several years.

Towards the end of the war, Ruth saw hundreds of gypsy families moving from the East to the West trying to escape the advancing Russian armies. Some of the gypsies were walking. Others, in gaily covered wagons loaded with all their possessions,

Ruth Brophy preparing to leave Linz for the U.S. in her native dress

played their musical instruments in an almost endless parade of humanity. Tens of thousands of gypsies had been victims of the German armies and now they were fleeing the Russians whom they feared as they had feared the Germans.

According to Ruth, the local railroad station had thousands of photographs posted on the walls of people desperately trying to locate family members, both civilians and military personnel who were missing. This, she reports, continued long after the war ended.

The U.S. Army had created special films of the victims of the Holocaust and required that the public be made aware of the atrocity of the Holocaust, which was still being denied by many civilians.

During the entire period of the war and the subsequent occupation by both the American and Russian armies, Ruth developed a very positive attitude about the American soldiers, and while she had no particular negative experiences with the Russian troops (she lived in the American zone), she knew from friends that the Austrian people really feared the Russians for many reasons, while they admired the attitude and helpfulness of the American service men.

Ruth told me that when the CIC staff occupied the family hotel, they were friendly and generous in supplying the family with government-issued food supplies. The friendship and actions of the troops became a major influence on her desire to live in the United States.

Ruth left for the United States in 1949 and her remarkable life story can be found on a fascinating website.*

Today, she has a loving family, a reputation as an outstanding artist and professional creator of websites. She is also aware and appreciative of the fulfilling life she has experienced and continues to enjoy.

---

* www.veryfineart.com

A German Diplomat Speaks

Note: Mr. Johannes Haas-Heye was a prominent German diplomat and member of the German resistance against The Third Reich. He wrote me a few short paragraphs, which I am pleased to share with my readers. My one regret is that I was unable to personally interview this remarkable 95-year-old gentleman who was subsequently honored by both the post-war German and Allied governments for his remarkable service during and after World War II.

Dear Mr. Satz,

My son, Christoph, told me that you are going to publish a book about your stay in postwar Austria 60 years ago. You saw most German and Austrian cities destroyed by bombs, because the Allies had expected to shorten the war, which would have been the case with a less fanatical population.

"Do you want the total war?" That's what Hitler's propaganda chief Goebbels had asked the Nazi crowd at the Sportpalast in Berlin in 1944. The arms went up and they roared their "Yes!" They got it, their total war and would certainly have retaliated against the Allies if their Luftwaffe had been what it was in 1939.

There was no hope left in Germany, but in 1948 came the currency reform. Business started. The American financial aid under the Marshall Plan helped a great deal, and reconstruction started on a tremendous scale.

The biggest help, however, was the Cold War. With mounting threats from the East, the Western powers became eager to help Germany along. In 1955, German was invited into NATO.

Sincerely,

Johannes Haas-Heye

United States Constabulary

W hen the war ended in Germany, there were 10 million displaced persons in Europe. Hundreds of thousands of allied soldiers awaited transportation home and discharge from the service. General chaos existed among the civilians of both the conquered and liberated countries, and there was little law and order anywhere. A critical need existed to create and implement a force of highly trained and skillfully organized individuals to rectify this situation.

While such an organization was discussed earlier among the allied commanders, it was not until Lt. General Joseph McNarvey, American military commander in Europe, appointed Major

Dress uniforms of U.S. Constabulary, 1946

Insignia of U.S. Forces Austria (USFA)

General Ernest Harmon to organize and command what turned out to be The United States Constabulary. This appointment was made in January of 1946.

Approximately 35,000 army personnel would become an elite force of highly trained troopers to oversee and manage complete control over both the military and civilian population. This highly trained force was implemented by July 1946 and consisted of the best soldiers, who volunteered to be trained as both policemen and soldiers and to be responsible for German civilians, American and allied personnel.

Their responsibility covered 16 million German civilians, over 500,000 refugees, and hundreds of thousands of American service men. The best equipment available was given to them and very special insignia was designed for their uniforms. They looked great and were known as "Lightning Police" or as often called, "The Circle-C-Cowboys."

Bill Billet at flag ceremony

By the time I was transferred from "H" company, 5th Infantry regiment in the fall of 1946, all but one, the 1st Infantry Division, of the wartime army combat divisions had either been returned to the U.S. or disbanded. In our area, it was the Constabulary who represented the U.S. Army.

Trouble With the Russians

Several times a week I played table tennis while visiting the Red Cross in Linz. There were five or six tables of round-robin competition. We usually played for 25 cents per game. Over a one-week period, we had an elimination tournament, and as I was a pretty good player, I was placed on the team designated as the alternate player of a four-person team. The following month found us on the Mozart Express, temporarily stopped at the Russian controlled border, waiting for clearance to travel through the Russian zone to the four-power controlled Vienna. We were to participate in a ping pong tournament.

A junior officer accompanied a Russian private as they went person-to-person with every individual on the train. When the five of us on the team presented our travel documents, the Russian asked us the purpose of our visit and to describe each of our assignments.

When told, he asked how many people participate at the same time— four or five? When we explained that there were single and double matches but never more than four competing at one time, the officer, smiled and asked, "Why are five men needed as a team?" Learning about the alternate, he asked us to identify that person (who was me) and said, "You all seem in good health. We will allow only four of you to pass through our checkpoint."

I was removed from the train and had to wait six hours for the next train heading back to Linz, missing my only opportunity to visit Vienna.

Displaced Persons: Search for a Family

In the summer of 1946, I had a meaningful experience in attempting to locate several families of displaced persons. A close friend of my mother wrote me that she had a cousin and her husband who were desperately trying to leave Austria from a displaced person facility and needed help as soon as possible. The only thing I knew were their names—Sarah and Joseph Jasnuski. Sarah was the only survivor of a huge Polish family of over 30 people who were killed by the Nazis.

For four weeks I used every source possible to locate them. I finally did at Camp Glasenbach, outside of Salzburg, Austria. Before I could meet them, I was given orders to lead a raid against a black market gang. I loaded a jeep with food, blankets, clothing, and some medical supplies and asked a good friend, Russ "Shorty" Andrews, to locate the family, give them the supplies and assure them that their relatives in Chicago would give them all the help necessary to bring them to the U.S.

Shorty took off and promised me that he would find them. Two days later, he returned with the news that he had met the

With "Shorty" Andrews, Ebelsburg,
Austria,1946

family and had given them the supplies. He even described them: Sarah looked about 30; Joseph looked close to 40; and there was a pretty little girl about 2. I appreciated Shorty's efforts.

The next week, I loaded up another jeep and made the trip myself. I arrived at the camp, which closely resembled a concentration camp. As I walked through the dirt, I loudly called Jasnuski's name. A man approached and explained that the Jasnuskis had left the camp. I insisted he was mistaken. The man insisted he wasn't. After all, he was Jasnuskis best friend, Samuel Rosenbaum. He said he was a lifetime friend. He claimed they went to school and religious services together. They married at the same time, and they went into the concentration camps together. The Jasnuski family had left this camp six weeks earlier. I realized at that moment that Shorty had deceived me. He had never seen the Jasnuskis and most likely sold the supplies that I gave him. I was furious.

Rosenbaum told me of a relative in Baltimore that he had been trying to contact to no avail. Would I post a letter? Perhaps the army mail would make a difference. I quickly agreed and suggested he deliver the letter to me at my hotel the following morning. That evening in my hotel, I was so angry about Shorty's deception that I couldn't sleep. At 11 p.m. I put on my raingear and walked outside. Sitting on the curb were Mr. and Mrs. Rosenbaum. They hadn't wanted to disturb me, but they were so determined that I get the letter that they were going to sit there all night.

The next day I returned to my base and Bob Noble, my first sergeant, told me that Shorty had been looking for me. When Noble told him I had gone to Glasenbach, Shorty knew the jig was up. He was a lying shit and later that week, asked for and got a transfer out of our company. I never saw him again.

Two additions to this episode: When I arrived in the U.S. months later, I called the Rosenbaum's relative in Baltimore. He told me to mind my own damn business and that Rosenbaum was a lousy parasite. Unbelievable.

About 15 years later I was attending a wedding in Chicago when a very small woman grabbed me, kissed and hugged me. and blurted out, "I'm Sarah Jasnuski! Oh, God bless you. I know all about you and what you tried to do for us."

The Jasnuskis had four daughters. Joseph was a successful businessman and they had achieved the American dream. When I asked them about the Rosenbaums, Sarah said, "Oh, they are very happy in Israel. Whenever they write, they ask, 'Have you met Lou yet? When you do, tell him how much we love him for what he tried to do for us.'" This incident was of great significance to me.

The Deer Hunter

One day, Mess Sergeant Herb Baker asked me if I would take a small detail and kill a deer for his famous deer stew, which he said the troops would really enjoy. It was late autumn and the deer-hunting season had just begun. First Sergeant Bob Noble picked three men, supposedly with hunting experience. He had already arranged hunting permits from the local game warden. We were issued German Mauser rifles (a .30 caliber rifle about two-thirds the length of our MI's) but very accurate for hunting game.

The day was sunny and cool. The foliage season was in full bloom and the forest we had entered was heavily wooded, with ample water for its inhabitants. The four of us jubilantly got into our jeep and went off on our big adventure.

I was in charge. Big deal! My entire hunting experience in Illinois was going quail hunting with my dad, armed with a .410 shotgun. I think I was 11 years old at the time and my dad was intent on making me into a macho man.

After we arrived at our destination, I knew enough to have the men set their watches properly with a time limit, enough to have them separate into a perpendicular line about 50 yards apart before we set off into the woods. I took the furthest point at the right of the column.

I loved tramping in the woods. I actually liked the feeling of power as I clutched my Mauser like a good friend. I remember the fragrance of the plant life and the sound of the very slight wind. I was having a great time. But suddenly I looked up as I heard a branch breaking and there it was, a giant buck. I think I counted a massive six-point antler. He was eating off a branch about 50 feet up away.

I felt an adrenalin rush, and with my heart pounding, I aimed just below his right shoulder, but at the last second, I raised my gun and shot into the air. I couldn't shoot that magnificent animal.

Within a few minutes, my three companions breathless arrived where I stood. I gasped, "He was huge—a six pointer!" And I motioned in the opposite direction to which he had run.

In 1978, I saw a Robert DeNiro film entitled "The Deer Hunter." When I saw this film, it immediately brought me back to my 1946 experience. Twice in the film DeNiro, by himself, is stalking a stag. The first time, he's totally self-assured, confident of his ability to kill this animal, and while respecting his prey, had no compunction in pulling the trigger. Several years later, after returning from the unbelievable madness of combat and the loss of his buddies, he again stalks a deer and simply cannot pull the trigger even though the animal is clearly in his sights. I felt an identity with the Robert DeNiro character.

A Fateful Event

One late afternoon in early October, I was in the orderly room when First Sergeant Bob Noble came in and asked me what I was doing there on Yom Kipper Eve instead of attending services. I explained that I was on duty and that there wasn't a synagogue within 60 kilometers. Sergeant Noble suggested that I get into his jeep and go up the road five kilometers to the Jewish displaced persons camp where he was certain they were conducting services. With that, Sgt. Noble tossed me the keys to his jeep and off I went. What a thoughtful man!

I drove to the DP camp. It had barbed wire fences, guard towers and heavy, unpleasant odors, dirt floors, and no privacy for the inmates. I walked towards a gathering of men only, led by an ancient rabbi in full orthodox regalia. Suddenly a young woman speaking fluent English wanted to know how I dared interrupt the services for which they had permission. In fact, I *had* interrupted the services. The rabbi suggested I lead them in prayers, but upon learning that I didn't know how, he insisted that I stand at his right elbow, a place of honor. I stood at his side and when the service was over, every single person in the camp, over 200 people, wished me a Happy New Year and hugged me. What an emotional feast! I was overwhelmed.

As long as I remained in Austria, when my workday was over, I went to the same DP camp. I brought food, clothing and medical supplies. I wrote many letters on behalf of the survivors to their relatives in the U.S. and I worked with a United Nations agency (UNRRA), whose mission was to relocate DPs and attempt to reunite families. Soon, some of my buddies were bringing in sheeting and plumbing supplies to help make the survivors lives more comfortable. It was a very meaningful experience and resulted in my lifetime personal interest in the Holocaust and its victims.

Many years later, when I was a publishing executive, the president of my company called me into his office and said, "Lou, next month one of the great heroes of the 20th century will be coming to NYC."

He was talking about Simon Weisenthal, hunter of Nazi war criminals that had committed horrible crimes against civilization. He had written the book *The Murderers Among Us*. This was Simon Weisenthal's memoir which would be published by McGraw-Hill, first in hardcover and later in paperback by my company, Bantam Books.

My assignment was to arrange a cocktail party for Weisenthal and the senior people of the two companies. When Weisenthal entered the room, he struck an imposing figure. You could feel the strength of this man. I was standing with about six people in a half circle when Weisenthal was brought to the group by the editorial chief. Each of them shook hands and exchanged pleasantries. But soon the two of us had a chance to talk.

"You know, Mr. Weisenthal, I've been to your country." I said.

"When? Where?" he asked.

I told him the story of Bob Noble and my experience on Yom Kippur. He looked at me quizzically and suddenly embraced me. There were tears streaming down his cheeks. "You were the young soldier who came to us that night?" he asked. "Do you know how you raised our spirits and gave us inspiration?"

The two of us embraced with strength and tenderness, and cried in the middle of a room filled with people. The event was one of the most meaningful, emotional nights of my life. I have related this incident many times and often people react with great emotion and often tears.

A Hero of the Ages

imon Weisenthal's story in many ways gives credence to the axiom "Truth is stranger than fiction." The horrors of his life, between being captured by the Gestapo in the summer of 1941 until his liberation from the Mauthausen concentration camp by the American army in 1945 almost defy believability.

Simon Weisenthal

He had survived imprisonment in 12 different concentration camps including five death camps. He was literally saved by minutes on several occasions and twice attempted suicide. He was told that his wife, Cyla, was killed. (She wasn't and her story of survival is also remarkable). These horrible experiences only increased his ability to survive and become the dedicated champion of justice.

As I wrote above, I did share Yom Kippur with him and 200 other Holocaust survivors at a displaced persons camp in Ebelsburg, Austria in October of 1946. At the service, he remembered a single American soldier and I, of course, knew nothing about Simon Weisenthal or his monumental effort to start a documentation center in Linz.

In spite of all the success Weisenthal had in furnishing vital information regarding war criminals that were still enjoying freedom, he had political problems and critics who denied his success. Perhaps some of these criticisms were warranted. Or maybe they stemmed from professional jealousy. Nevertheless, they caused disappointment and frustration to Weisenthal and his co-workers. Still, his accomplishments were undeniable.

When Terry Davis, chairman of the Council of Europe, learned of Weisenthal's death, he said, "Without Simon Weisenthal's relentless effort to find Nazi criminals and bring them to justice and to fight anti-Semitism and prejudice, Europe would never have succeeded in healing its wounds and reconciling itself. He was a soldier of justice, which is indispensable to our freedom, stability and peace."

The Holocaust: Its Horrors and Heroes

In 1944, during my first year at the University of Illinois, my fraternity, Phi Epsilon Pi, welcomed Abraham Sacher as an honorary member. Abe was the director of Hillel Foundation, a Jewish cultural and spiritual organization that was created at the University in 1923. Subsequently, he became the founding president of Brandeis University and wrote one of the most memorable books, *Redemption of the Unwanted*, a classic history of the refugees of the Holocaust.

Every Sunday morning Abe came to our fraternity house for breakfast, followed by fascinating discussions on every conceivable subject. For many of us, it was the high spot of the week.

Then in April 1945 came the liberation of the Dachau concentration camp, one of Hitler's most infamous death camps. When Abe spoke about this event, shock and grief hit us all. I, for one, experienced disbelief and unmitigated anger. At that time, I had no idea that one year later I would be personally affected by this horrific event.

Obviously, I wasn't alone in my feelings of anger and desolation. Major General "Hollywood" Harry Collins, too, felt fury and anger and his determination knew no bounds. It was his division, the 42nd Rainbow that liberated Dachau.

During the liberation, General Collins formed a relationship with a young Jewish chaplain, Captain Eli A. Bohnen, who was one of the first American liberators.

General Collins assured Chaplain Bohnen that there would be no limit on medical supplies, food, clothing, housing and efforts to locate family survivors. He, as both military and civilian commander, brought in the local civilian population to clean up the camp. Most of these local people denied any knowledge of the atrocities that occurred there. It was later learned that General Collins went way beyond his own area of responsibility to aid the survivors. He was a man of great compassion and totally result oriented.

Chaplain Bohnen entered the Army in 1943 after graduating from the Jewish Theological Seminary in New York City. The following is a description of his experiences taken from a letter he wrote to his wife, Eleanor, on May 1, 1945.

Nothing you can put in words would adequately describe what I saw there. The human mind refuses to believe what the eyes see. All the stories of Nazi horrors are underestimated rather than exaggerated. We saw freight cars with bodies in them. The people had been transported from one camp to another, and it had taken about a month for the train to make the trip. In all that time, they had not been fed. They were lying in grotesque positions, just as they had died. Many were naked, others in thin clothing. But all were horrible to see.

We entered the camp itself and saw the living. The Jews were the worst off. Many of them looked worse than the dead. They cried as they saw us. I spoke to a large group of Jews. I don't remember what I said. I was under a mental strain, but Heimberg (my assistant) tells me that they cried as I spoke. Some of the people were crying all the time we were there. They were emaciated, diseased, beaten, miserable caricatures of human beings. I don't know how they didn't all go mad. There were thousands and thousands of prisoners in the camp. Some of them didn't look too bad but most looked terrible. And as I said, the Jews were the worst. Even the other prisoners who suffered miseries themselves couldn't get over the horrible treatment meted out to the Jews.

I shall never forget what I saw, and in my nightmares, the scenes recur. When I got back, I couldn't eat and I couldn't even muster up enough energy to write you. No possible punishment would ever repay the ones who were responsible.

Many years later, my company, Bantam Books, along with NBC television, would simultaneously publish and present *Holocaust*, the novel written by Gerald Greene. The 9 1/2-hour TV series would ultimately gain a huge international audience.

It was my responsibility to establish national and international distribution for the book. We sent letters and promotional support to over 1,000 customers indicating what we thought their allocation should be. We also gave each customer an opportunity to change the quantity we had suggested if they had good reason to do so.

A few days after we made the solicitation, one of my staff approached me with a strange look on his face. "Look, Lou, this is really something. Look at the Philadelphia order." The United News Company, a highly successful periodical distribution company that also operated a fleet of trucks covering a huge territory, had changed its allocation from 5,000 to 60,000 copies. I was astonished and said to my associate, "I gotta call Sid."

Sid Stern, the owner, and a long-standing customer and friend of mine, never gave me a chance to even say hello. "If you give me one copy less of *Holocaust*, I'll never sell another copy of any book you publish."

"Why do you want so many copies, Sid?" I asked.

He replied, "Because I was in the advance company of the 42nd Rainbow Division that liberated Dachau. What I saw was too horrific to describe. Some of us guys were so sickened that we were immobilized and couldn't think straight," Sid continued. "It took hours, and for some of us, days, before we fully recovered. Some guys never did. So, Lou, when your 60,000 copies of *Holocaust* come into my distribution center, every school, library, bookstore, supermarket, drug chain, liquor store, bus, train and airport newsstand, every conceivable outlet that sells a book, magazine or newspaper will display your book, and I will fully support it with my own promotional expenses.

"Every person in my territory," said Sid, "will be aware of this book and TV presentation because this disaster should never be forgotten."

We sent him the 60,000 copies. Sid was true to his word.

Earlier in this chapter, I wrote about Major General Harry Collins and his relationship with the Jewish chaplain, Captain Eli Bohnen. This was an amazing blending of two totally committed and passionate men who came from two widely different cultural backgrounds and under almost impossible circumstances made monumental efforts (and results) to support the survivors of the Dachau concentration camp.

The allied high command, the American congress and administration, the newly established United Nations Relief Organization, the World Jewish Community and particularly the

Child's drawing of Major General Harry Collins

victorious armies had no concept of the enormity of the problem. Collectively, they had to resolve the problems of the 10 million displaced individuals, including the survivors of the Holocaust.

Possibly I used General Collins as an example because on four separate occasions I interacted on a personal level with the general. There were virtually no instructions to our military leaders of what they should do to try and resolve these issues.

In Germany and Austria as the concentration camps were being liberated by the American army, about 30 American Jewish chaplains, mostly junior grade officers, took the responsibility and necessary actions to bring relief to the victims.

These chaplains, without regard to their own personal safety and careers, brought food, clothing, medical supplies, forged official documents, wrote thousands of letters to seek help and attempt to reconcile families. They petitioned their congressmen, helped raise millions of dollars from every resource possible, and in plain words, they made a huge difference.

It should also be noted that many of these chaplains also greatly influenced their senior commanders to "look the other way" while they were getting the job done. I hesitate to mention any other single person or acts of courage enacted by these heroic chaplains, but Abraham Klausner, a reformed rabbi, performed his responsibilities with unbelievable accomplishments. He literally saved thousands of lives and helped create significant improvements for many thousands of victims from many different countries and religions.

Displaced persons camp, Ebelsburg, Austria 1945
Courtesy of Joseph and Rachel Greenfield

Up to now, my feelings about General Collins have been totally positive. But I want to write about an incident, which was referred to as "The Gold Train," part of a book, *Spoils of World War II* published by Birchland Press.

Apparently 24 railroad cars filled with paintings, gold and silver antiques and jewelry, valued at over 200 million dollars, were confiscated from Hungarian Jewish families on the way to concentration camps. The train was high jacked and subsequently "guarded" by American personnel under the command of General Collins.

Some officers "borrowed" some of these treasures and it was thought that General Collins had masterminded this incident. None of these allegations were ever proven and virtually all of these treasures were recovered and distributed through various agencies of the United Nations to survivors of the Holocaust and their families.

In recent years, an additional 30 million dollars were distributed to Hungarian Jews who had proven that their families had lost these valuables. I believe that with this settlement, the issue was put to rest. I don't believe that this incident will harm the reputation of General Collins when his record as one of America's World War II heroes is evaluated.

I do remember, however, that on Christmas Eve 1946, two buddies, three Red Cross women, and I serenaded the general. We were invited into his home to sing Christmas carols with him. The six of us were overwhelmed when we entered the house. It was like an enchanted palace. No one questioned his taste in furnishings, but did wonder how he had acquired all that luxury.

My Paris Adventure

Marvin Spira is a lifelong friend. We first met as 4 year olds. We were neighbors in Chicago. We went to grammar school, high school, and were roommates at the University of Illinois. We even entered military service at the same time. Although we now see each other infrequently, we remain in constant touch and consider ourselves brothers.

In early October, Marv was stationed at Orly Field, a huge air force base outside of Paris. I reached him by telephone from Ebelsburg, Austria, and arranged to meet him in Paris. We met the first evening at the Arch de Triumph and found it unbelievable that the two kids from Rogers Park, Chicago, were there together.

When I left Marv that evening to return to my hotel, he asked me to be at Orly Field at 8 a.m. the following day. I balked at the thought of getting up that early but for some strange reason he insisted. At 8 a.m. I went to the main gate and was sent to see the Provost Marshal. He instructed me to grab an armband, special helmet, and a 45 automatic pistol. When I asked what was going on, the Provost Marshal just smiled.

Five minutes later I stood on the edge of the field with 23 other men. A huge cargo plane landed and taxied to where we stood in formation. A gang-plank-type stairway was put in place. Striding down the stairs came (1) a one-star general; (2) a four-star general —General Lucius Clay, Supreme Commander of the Allied Forces (who replaced General Dwight Eisenhower); and, (3) Secretary of State James Byrnes, recently appointed by President Truman. They came to the Luxemburg Palace to represent the U.S. along with our allies from China, France, Russia, Great Britain, and top officials of many other countries. The Luxemburg Peace Conference was one of the most significant postwar meetings of the four major powers.

My 23 fellow soldiers and I had been selected to be the honor guard to Secretary Byrnes and for two days we performed this duty. It was fascinating as well as historical. The Secretary of State personally thanked each of us when the duty ended. Most of our duties were ceremonial events. We were kind of window dressing representing our country and looking very "spiffy."

Two days later, Marv was given four box seats to the opera, hosted by France's president and prime minister. The following night we saw Faust, performed with over 100 top diplomats and general officers present, some with very attractive women in full evening dress. Even Marv brought two beautiful young women, attired in smashing formal gowns. They were both officers in the nurse corps.

During intermission, while Marv and his date adjourned to the main lobby, my companion and I stood to stretch our legs. As I looked around the hall, I could hardly believe that I was in one of the most famous opera houses in the world and at such an historic time. Looking up at the box directly above, I saw Vyacheslav

Molotov, the Foreign Minister of Russia. We made direct eye contact; he smiled at my companion and me and gave me a double-thumbs up.

Licensed brothels were an integral part of Paris history. But I had learned the week before arriving in Paris that a new law had been passed prohibiting prostitution even in licensed brothels. So when Marv and I would split up in the evenings to return to our respective lodgings, I wasn't surprised to see 15 to 20 prostitutes standing near the entrance to my hotel. Up to then, these women had been protected by law and were even given free medical care. Many of them were special friends to men in the highest social circles. Now they were out in the street, thousands of them, mostly young and attractive. And they were aggressively soliciting members of the armed forces.

I was fascinated. I noticed one woman, very young and attractive who appeared extremely shy and never approached any of the men. After noticing her for a few evenings, I was surprised when she walked over to me, smiled and, in excellent English asked if we could talk. I learned that her name was Giacento, and that she had come from Corsica.

She had been a telephone operator, and was engaged to be married. In desperate financial straits, Giacento and her fiancé agreed that she should go to Paris for six months and become a prostitute. No sooner had she arrived in Paris than the laws changed. She was on the street.

She gathered her courage and asked me to go with her to her apartment. I was a 19-year-old kid with very little sexual experience. I agreed to spend the evening with her but had no intention of sleeping with her. The very prospect frightened me.

Feeding French children

I suggested we get something to eat. She took me to an all-night café and introduced me to escargot, a delicacy I never knew existed. We ate and talked for almost two hours and I was thoroughly enjoying her company, so much so that my apprehension eased and my sexual desire grew. She persuaded me that we would be good together. Her room was a fifth floor walk up. While very small and dimly lit, it was spotlessly clean and inviting. I will never forget the next few hours. Our lovemaking was wonderful, tender and passionate. When I left, we hugged and kissed and as I walked down the stairs I was filled with gratitude.

Marv's Story

Author's note: France, Germany and Austria were classified in different categories. Germany was conquered; Austria was first classified as conquered, then switched to liberated by the Allied High Command. But France was liberated. Because of this difference in classification, I thought France would certainly warrant a special section in my book, and I'm fortunate to have Marvin Spira, my lifelong friend who spent his entire overseas duty in France during the same time period I was stationed in Germany and Austria, write some of his experiences and observations of his duty. The following was written by Marv, and I hope it will give readers a different perception of occupation duty during 1945 and 1946.

W e landed at Le Havre, France, in late September of 1945 after a 10-day journey from Fort Hamilton, in Brooklyn, N.Y.

We were assigned to tents and told we were being re-assigned from the 10th Air Force (B-24 bombers) to the Air Transport Command. No more need for heavy bombers.

While at Le Havre, we ate out of mess kits and did little else but eat, sleep and wait for our transportation to be arranged. My first and very unforgettable perception of the war was seeing children, ages 4 to 10, crowding around the garbage cans near the mess halls, grabbing whatever food scraps they could get and running off, cramming the scraps into their mouths.

I kept going back to fill my mess kit up again with food and tried to give it to the children. I succeeded for the first few times until an officer came up to me and reprimanded me for doing it. He claimed it was establishing an act that would be replicated by others and that the children would become dependant on this manner of obtaining food. When I said, "Good! Let them eat clean food," I was again commanded to stop this activity. I will never forget the children's faces, scrounging in the garbage.

Fortunately, within a few days, we were loaded on a train bound for Paris, and then by truck transport to Orly Field on the outskirts of Paris. It was one in the morning. We rode through the

Army nurses in France

empty streets of Paris, seeing sights I had only viewed in magazines or postcards. For me, it was thrilling and exciting, a feeling that never left me until I was sent home.

In 1945 and 1946, I was assigned to the military police at Orly Field. One of my assignments was to teach the French police basic English so they could work with the U.S. military police, at least in basic military and police parlance. My French was fairly fluent at the time and I enjoyed the assignment. The relationship afforded me the opportunity to understand the feeling between the French, the military and the American occupying forces.

Marv Spira at gravesite of cousin, Lt. Marty Fried,
who in 1944 was shot down over France.

At first, the gratitude was heartwarming and graciously accepted. I made friends easily with many of my colleagues and was able to discuss their views and concepts of the war. They felt that the U.S Army was a major factor in saving their country and assisting them to return to a normal pre-war existence.

The Nazi occupation of France, and in particular Paris, was a hateful occurrence and one that the French fought hard, both emotionally and physically, to end. They felt that they would have overturned the Nazi forces but that the allied armies hastened that result.

Less than one year later, the feeling began to be one of resentment and impatience toward the average GI. And the independent nationalistic French spirit began to take hold. There were many conflicts between American soldiers and French civilians, and both the French gendarmerie and the U.S. military police were being taxed in smoothing out these conflicts.

The feeling of resentment stemmed from our presence in France and our "interfering" with their way of life. The French felt that after all, the war was over, and we've been through this many times before. Now let us get on with our own lives again.

I discussed this change in attitude with my many French friends and colleagues and they all came to the same conclusion: "Thanks for helping us and getting us back on our feet but now go home, leave us and our families alone and don't interfere in a country about which you have no real feeling."

When Charles de Gaul took over the government, the provincial or nationalistic feeling was even more emphasized. By the time I left Paris (December 1946), it was relatively uncomfortable to be involved. I had many close friends and families with whom I had warm relationships, and as individual associations had nothing but very pleasant times. As a whole, however, I could see and feel the coming resentment, as is probably natural when visiting people come to assist in the redevelopment of a country. This attitude was, of course, quite different in Germany, where a nation had been conquered and was being occupied as a result of the war.

I was very fortunate being stationed at Orly Field in Paris, because I was able to be in the center of the city at least three or four times a week. One weekend, about November of 1945, I was on the Champs Elysee walking with a large crowd towards the Arch de Triumph. I asked what the occasion was and was told that in a few hours, towards dusk, the lights were to be turned on for the first time in over four years, illuminating this magnificent monument.

I moved with the crowd and was able to get a spot on the street about 200 yards away from the arch. A parade of armed forces and equipment kept flowing and band after band marched past. About 4:30 p.m., bands circled the arch, and a black Citroen drove up near the arch. Dignitaries and government and army officials had been gathering. The crowd was relatively quiet.

General Charles de Gaul stepped out of the black Citroen and proceeded to a small platform on one side of the arch. There was a long rope suspended from the top of the arch, and secured to the platform on which de Gaul and other dignitaries were standing. At 5:15 p.m., all the bands began playing the Marseilles. Bright lights flooded the arch.

De Gaul pulled on the rope, and the tri-color dropped down from the top of the arch. The entire crowd was singing the Marseilles, I along with them. Tears were abundant and mine mingled with theirs.

And then I thought, what was a 19-year-old kid like me doing in the middle of the Champs Elysee in Paris, France, participating in one of the most emotional moments in French history?

I had that same feeling many times over while I was in France— the opening of the opera and the art galleries. An evening salon with Jean Paul Sartre; the opening of a prize bottle of cognac hidden for five years in a small café. I will always be thankful that I was able to recognize occasions and experiences that will live with me forever.

There was a small hole-in-the-wall tailor shop located at Orly Field, Paris in 1945. The tailor's name was Leon Szutenson.

He did excellent and quick work on the jackets and pants I would bring in to be cut to size. (I always asked for the uniforms two sizes larger than necessary so that Leon could tailor them to be form fitting). He was always very quiet and polite, and one day, as I was picking up a jacket, I heard him, very softly mutter, " Bist du a Yid?" (Are you Jewish?). I looked up in surprise and with a big smile on my face, I said "Yah, ich bin auch a Yid." (Yes, I am also Jewish). He grinned, and at the same time, a tear trickled down his face. He said, in half Yiddish and half French, "I didn't know if there were many of us left, anywhere."

Leon had had a very successful custom tailor shop in Paris, and a very nice home in the suburbs of Paris, called Ris Orangis. He lived there with his wife Rachele, his daughter, son-in-law and their two children, a baby boy, 1 year old and a daughter 6 years old. One night, his neighbors knocked on his door and said the Nazis were coming through the suburbs and taking all the Jewish families away and there was little or no time to prepare.

Leon conferred with his family and they decided to split up and flee to friends' houses in the country. Their daughter and son-in-law took the baby, some clothes and supplies and left within the hour. Leon and his wife took the granddaughter and left about two hours later, after hurriedly hiding a few family valuables in their basement.

Leon and his wife hid in a friend's farmhouse for about 14 months until the war ended. When they returned to their house in Ris Orangis, they found that it was still intact. The neighbors had watched over it for them hoping some day they might return. Leon never heard from his daughter or son-in-law, nor was he able to trace them after they parted.

His tailor shop in Paris was gone, and he was not able to reclaim any part of his shop or goods, which had been taken over by French citizens after the Nazis left Paris.

Leon, Rachele, and his little granddaughter Sarah, and I became good friends. I visited them frequently in their home, and spent many comfortable evenings teaching Sarah English. And to Leon, I explained the role of the United States, and the armed forces in liberating Europe and told him about the concentration camps. His fragmented information made him feel that he might be one of the very few Jews left in Europe.

After leaving France, I maintained a correspondence with Leon and his family and visited him in 1948 when I returned for a few months. By then, Leon had opened a small custom tailor shop in the suburbs and was able to live relatively comfortably. I lost touch with him in the mid 50s.

A New Career for Lou

When I returned from Paris, I was ordered to report to Major General Harry Collins. He invited me into his office and put me at ease. We chatted about Paris. I had no idea why I was in front of the general or what in the world he wanted. After a few comments about Paris, the general indicated that he was interested in borrowing the complete set of *The Lives and Loves of Frank Harris* that he had heard I recently acquired.

I had, in fact, for $5 obtained the notorious four-volume erotic adventures of the well-known New York Herald Tribune journalist who in the 1890s lived and worked in Paris. I confirmed that I had the set, and the general asked if I would bring it to him immediately. Within 10 minutes, the four-volume set was on the general's desk and I never saw the books again.

Major changes had been made in my absence. The 5th Infantry Regiment was merged into the 24th Constabulary Squadron at Ebelsburg, and the 4th Constabulary Squadron was stationed at

Masthead of *The New Cavalier*, November 1946

Wells. Troops of these units were posted at seven other towns throughout the American occupation zone of Austria, conducting law and order and security missions.

When I received the orders for my new assignment, I was shocked and dismayed. I was assigned to a radio/communications center situated in the mountains about 10 kilometers from Ebelsburg. I was to be in charge of that facility with a detail of three men to assist me. I felt I had far greater capabilities than this job required.

Before I was to start, I saw a sign posted on the regimental headquarters bulletin board requesting any person with newspaper publishing experience to report to Captain Barr who was stationed in Linz at our principal headquarters. My rationale for applying for this assignment was that I could read, type, and even then had a major interest in sports and international politics. Also, my three semesters at the University of Illinois were a real asset.

Apparently, I impressed Captain Barr, who during a 10-minute interview, told me about General Collins' orders to publish a weekly newspaper to glorify the cavalry. I got the position. My assignment was that of editor and general manager of *The New Cavalier*, a weekly newspaper.

Major General Harry Collins was one of General George Patton's favorite officers and possibly the most flamboyant commander of the 3rd Army Corps. The general not only wanted our newspaper to glorify the cavalry but to endear him to the local population as well. He wanted to become the "MacArthur" of the European occupation.

General Collins was a huge man, close to 220 pounds and well over six feet tall. His grey hair was closely cropped and he stood straight as a ramrod. His own commanders feared him almost as much as did the top generals of the Wehrmacht and SS Armies who he continually defeated in battle. General Collins was also totally respected and feared by the top Russian generals and he was a master player in the developing the Cold War with our Russian allies.

Captain Barr, who had interviewed me, advised me that he was going home the following week and that I should now meet his successor who occupied the next office down the corridor. I knocked on the door and received a reply to come in. Imagine my shock and joy to see Captain John Carley sitting at his desk with a great smile on his face. "Welcome, Satz! Do you think I would waste your talents sitting on your behind doing nothing at the top of a mountain? I selected you for this job as soon as I received my new assignment."

When I started my new assignment, I was told I could pick any seven members of the command to assist me in managing the newspaper. I would have a photographer, a driver, four editorial people and an assistant. We took over new headquarters with private sleeping quarters for my staff.

We were given an open checkbook. Anything we needed or wanted we could have. The assignment was to produce the newspaper by Thanksgiving. This was October 15th and I knew nothing about publishing a weekly newspaper. I knew nothing about printing, engraving, editorial, and so forth. We had only German-speaking suppliers and my staff was as ignorant as I about what we were doing—or supposed to be doing.

We made every mistake possible, yet we had great fun. It was a primitive process but we succeeded with sheer bravado, and now Andy, my assistant, and I were at the bindery watching the entire printing of 16,000 copies coming off the press. It was Thanksgiving eve.

As we watched these copies coming off the belt, I realized with great distress that we had not thought about how the newspapers would be distributed. I had a moment of panic until an idea came to me. I had come to know Major Frank Fitzpatrick, chief chaplain of the entire command. I knew that he had at his command 25 chaplain assistants, each of whom had a vehicle. I immediately contacted Father Fitzpatrick, explained the situation, and within three hours, the newspapers were loaded into 25 three-quarter ton vehicles. By 9 a.m. the next day, the entire printing had been delivered to 25 distribution centers. We had accomplished our mission.

Thanksgiving 1946

It had been many months since the war in Europe ended but conditions in Austria were chaotic. Cities were still clearing debris from the Allied bombings, and the infrastructure was literally starting all over. The Cold War with Russia was heating up on a daily basis and civilian morale was low. Moreover, the morale of the American troops had hit bottom. Most of the combat troops had been rotated back to civilian life leaving young, inexperienced kids and a relative handful of junior officers and regular army noncommissioned officers responsible for maintaining the monumental tasks of the army of occupation. The troops were overworked, bored and unappreciated by the local population. Our troops were also not very well disciplined.

In this environment, the members of the 5th Infantry Regiment were at the very end of the extensive supply line and they could not remember the last time they had a piece of fresh fruit or vegetable or a drink of milk. Thus, they were looking forward to Thanksgiving Day.

The mess sergeant, Herb Baker, a farm boy from Iowa, decided to make a difference. No one knows how he did it, but Herb brought in dozens of turkeys, delicious hams, sides of fresh beef, potatoes (both mashed and sweet), cranberry sauce, fresh beans, home-baked rolls, apple and pumpkin pies and all kinds of soft drinks. The beer came later at the PX. We were billeted in the former German Luftwaffe headquarters for officers. Our mess hall was in the basement of the building and had eight half-windows. As 160 men prepared to sit down to dinner, every window of the mess hall revealed at least one wide-eyed youngster peering in, filled with surprise and envy.

"Get those kids in here!" Baker yelled. In two minutes about 15 boys between 8 and 12 stood quivering in fear in front of Baker. Speaking fluent German, he said: "OK, kids, I'm going to give you 30 minutes to bring your families, neighbors, friends and anybody else you can find, and you'll all get the best meal of your lives. Now scram, *mach schnell* (real fast)!"

Thirty minutes later, more than 60 civilians, at first in disbelief, then in total joy were surrounded by 160 equally happy GIs for a wonderful shared feast.

Afterward, news of the feast got out to the community and for weeks later housewives were not only bringing fresh bakery goods but fresh fruit and vegetables to our troops. Our guys started local baseball and football teams (American-style) with the kids, and their local spiritual leaders invited their men to join in the activities. A whole new community was created.

The goodwill created Thanksgiving Day was far more effective than the entire efforts of the official government. No one who attended this event would ever forget it. Photographs taken that day were reproduced in *Stars & Stripes*, and then sent to the national wire service. This was the American GIs at their very best.

Mistaken Identity

Andy O'Brien, my assistant while managing *The New Cavalier*, came into my office and told me that in two weeks we would be completely out of newsprint. This would mean the end of our jobs.

That same day, I met Major Fitzpatrick, our chaplain, who suggested I call Al Benecke for some help. Benecke was an administrator and purchasing agent stationed in the American sector of Vienna. We had a very efficient telephone operator who within 10 minutes had Benecke on the telephone.

To this day, I don't know what got into me at that particular moment— maybe fear of losing our great jobs— but I opened our conversation as follows: "Benecke, I'm Sergeant Satz, general manager of *The New Cavalier*, which is the general's pride and joy. We need newsprint now or we're out of business and the general will be furious. How fast can you get me our requirements?"

Silence.

"Do you hear me, Benecke?"

"Let me understand what you're saying. You're Sergeant Satz, general manager of *The New Cavalier?*"

"Right!"

"You need newsprint immediately to maintain operation of *The New Cavalier*?"

"Right. You got it! And we need the newsprint— now!"

"Okay. I have three things to tell you: One: My name is **Colonel** Al Benecke.

Two: You'll get your damned newsprint within three days. And Three: How would you like to come to Vienna and work for me?"

Silence. (I was dumbfounded.)

"So, Sergeant Satz? I can't hear you."

"Thank you very much, sir, I really appreciate your assistance on behalf of *The New Cavalier* but I'm scheduled for discharge within the next month so I can't accept your generous offer."

Civilian Relationships

It was not easy to get acquainted with many civilians. Leopoldina Klima was an exception. She was in her late 40s, never married and an excellent secretary to our battalion commander, who gave us access to her administrative talents. She worked out of our office. Lee, as we called her, spoke fluent English and was generous in helping some of us learn basic words and idioms in German. She read voraciously and loved classical music.

One day she hesitantly asked me if she could write a letter to my mother. I didn't ask why but said yes. (It turned out she liked me because I was respectful.) This began a correspondence that continued long after I returned home. Her spirits were tremendously uplifted each time she received a letter or package from my mother. Lee introduced me to the works of Anton Bruckner, especially his choral works, one of which I attended at the Salzburg Music Festival.

Joseph Gangleberg was another story. He became my interpreter when I managed *The New Cavalier*. Gangleberg was 26 years old, an ex- major in the SS Ski Corps on the Russian front and a very personable man. He continuously attempted to teach me to ski and take hikes into the mountains. He also wanted to introduce me to young women.

I made it very clear to him, however, that being an SS officer meant, first of all, that he was a Nazi. Not only did he volunteer for military service, he embraced it. And as far as I was concerned, ours was a business only arrangement.

In later years, realizing how many ex Nazis achieved major positions in the new German and Austrian governments, I felt I had possibly missed some good opportunities for broadening my knowledge and pleasure, but at that time I was so overwhelmed with anger because of the horrors of the Holocaust, I simply couldn't consider Gangleberg as a potential friend.

Christmas Party in Linz

I t was Christmas Eve 1946. As the editor and general manager of *The New Cavalier*, I had been asked to help coordinate 350 simultaneous Christmas parties for all the children of Austria. I was to coordinate the parties with the American Red Cross and the Chaplain Corps. The Christmas party in Linz turned out to be the largest of the 350 parties and we were totally exhausted when the children left the Red Cross building about 9 p.m. on Christmas Eve.

In Linz, I would estimate that we entertained about 500 to 600 children from ages 3 to 16. The quartermaster corps supplied the hot dogs, hamburgers, ice cream, soft drinks and potato chips. The Red Cross had organized baking parties, which included some local housewives and many young women who served as hostesses at the club.

All the young people enjoyed the small games and toys, which were partially paid for by the PX managers. Many servicemen made personal contributions for the festivities.

We provided puppet shows and some movie comedies and cartoons. Hundreds of GIs participated in playing with the

Children's Christmas party, Linz, Austria 1946

children, and many of the troops went to late evening mass. It was really an incredible event.

Joy Andrews, local head of the Red Cross, thanked us for a job well done and suggested we go outside, as she had arranged a surprise for us. Outside the Red Cross entrance were three one-horse open sleighs, jingle bells, and all. The night was crystal clear, thousands of stars in the skies, and falling snow covered the ground. Each of us guys bundled with three nifty Red Cross women and drove off into the woods.

After about 15 minutes of riding, we spotted a huge castle, which was the home of General Harry Collins. The six of us left our sleighs and started to serenade the general. After the first song, the door of the castle opened and an aide of the general invited us in for drinks and sweets. There was General Collins, dressed in lederhosen shorts, high socks and a beautiful brocade shirt. He went to the piano and with an excellent tenor voice led us in several songs. We left after a half-hour, our hearts filled with joy and warmth.

At 3:30 that morning, I was awakened by a strange voice. "Satz! Get up now! You're going home!" What a fantastic way to end my overseas duty. But it wasn't all that easy.

Ship of Shame

A nightmare that lasted almost a full month had begun. About 15 of us were trucked to the rail center where approximately 200 men were assembled. We piled on to 40x 8s, unheated boxcars that during World War I accommodated 40 men or eight horses. It took us two days to arrive

Ponta Delgada· Açores

SS General Stuart Heintzelman, 1945-1954

at a huge airfield in Bremerhaven, Germany. There, we were billeted with about 2,000 men in each of several hangars which had formerly housed aircraft of the German Luftwaffe. The air temperature was zero degrees Fahrenheit, aided by a wind chill factor of 20 below. We spent a miserable New Year's Eve awaiting orders.

The week of January 2nd, 1,500 troops were trucked to the Port of Bremerhaven, where the USS General Stuart Heintzelman was moored, awaiting our arrival. As we boarded the Heintzelman, some of the guys patted the ship's rail enthusiastically and said, "Hey, this is the baby that's going to take us home!"

"Don't be so damn sure, buddy," one crewman said. "We've tried three times so far, and we never made it. You're on a jinxed ship. Be careful." We laughed at him as we boarded.

Our quarters were in the foul smelling hold of the ship with four pieces of canvas tied to steel railings, which provided four bunks for sleeping. We had no place to store our belongings.

The first day, MPs were stationed at the water fountains; we were limited to water twice a day. Showers were out of the question, and for the first few days, nobody really cared. The first meal was totally inedible, and later in the evening, two men from the mess hall sold us peanut butter sandwiches for $3 each. Virtually all of us paid the price.

After the first night I turned lucky. I sought out one of the junior officers of the ship to volunteer and get the job of editing the ship's daily newspaper. This mimeographed two-page daily provided various instructions and some not very funny jokes. More important, I prepared a daily graph for the troops to show how far we had traveled that day and how many miles we still had to go. We were scheduled to arrive in New York nine days from departure.

And best of all, I was given a cot, typewriter, and mimeograph machine a few feet from the bridge and use of the crew's latrine, thus avoiding the smelly hold where the rest of the troops were quartered.

By the time we left the North Sea, the seas were shaking the ship so badly that many men became seasick. That condition worsened daily as we entered the North Atlantic. Each day I would get a reading from the bridge telling us where we were and how far we had traveled. We experienced waves of 25 to 30 feet, and it didn't take me long to figure out that we were losing distance and slowly, painfully working our way south rather than west to New York City.

Virtually all of the Army personnel and some crew members were seasick, and conditions down in the hold were getting unbearable. I saw crashing waves pick up crewmen and smash them against bulkheads, breaking their bones.

I had a friend down below who had come up to see me several times. When I didn't see him for over two days, I went down to look for him. I found him, lying in his own waste under the bottom of his four-tier bunk. He was semi-conscious and almost in shock when I discovered him. Fortunately, he recovered.

Each day we went further south and conditions became more and more intolerable. Food remained inedible and a food strike ensued that caused several serious injuries. It took the MPs over an hour to quell the strike. A woman officer was assaulted and no one was found responsible for that horrible crime. There were 150 African American GI's aboard and we experienced a race war instigated by several stupid red necks. Three or four injuries occurred and tension on the ship became unbearable.

During the voyage, I'd noticed an increase in minor arguments that a few of the southern red necks had with some of the African American troops. There were snide remarks but no major incidents.

I'm not certain what kicked off what turned out to be a major scuffle, but I do remember many African American men, a few who flashed knives, crowded together on one deck and then many of the Caucasian troops close by shouting racial insults, which got uglier every minute. A few from each side started to push and scream. One or two pulled out their knives but were quickly disarmed by either their own comrades or MPs who rushed in to stop the fight.

Although this particular incident was not repeated, as a witness I admit to being very frightened because it seemed that just about everything on this voyage was going wrong with no indication that circumstances would improve.

In addition to all this, the sea was on a rampage and many of us feared that we were going to capsize. The captain of the Queen Mary, also in these same waters at that time, was later quoted in Life magazine as saying, "It was the worst and most dangerous crossing I have ever experienced."

One night when I went to bed the crashing of the waves and the crazy movements of the ship made me think it might be all over for us. But I fell into a fitful sleep and when I awakened in the morning, I thought I had died and gone to heaven. We were anchored in Ponte Del Gada in the Azores Islands, a tropical paradise off the cost of Portugal.

As I dashed out to the deck, I saw a beautiful harbor lined with palm trees, and pastel-shade houses. Fisherman in small boats sent up empty baskets to us in which we put money. The baskets were lowered, and in turn, the fisherman sent up sardines, fresh fruit and breads in the baskets. They undoubtedly took advantage of us but we were starved.

Later that day, the senior military officer of our group gave shore leave to half of the troop that numbered 1,500. When these stir-crazy guys hit the shore, all hell broke loose—drinking to excess, setting fires, and chasing women along the shoreline. Sirens screamed and general chaos hit the island. The shore patrol gathered troop members into nets and dumped the guys on to our deck. Motor launches brought in the balance of the troops, and some time later that day, a coast guard aircraft brought in two coast guard commanders who took over operations of the ship.

Although I never went ashore during this event, I saw the smoke and fires, heard the screams of women and the sirens of police and fire engines. And again, I asked myself, "What else could possibly go wrong?"

Fresh food and supplies from an American airbase on Ponte Del Garda were brought in and military police brought order to the troops. The MPs remained on the ship. No more shore leave was granted.

We understood that the captain, the chief mess officer, and a mess employee were confined to their cabins. We were told that help was on its way and a major investigation by top authorities would take place as quickly as possible. The two coast guard commanders continued to control and manage the ship.

Several days later, the USS General MB Stewart, sister ship of the Heintzelman that had left Bremerhaven for New York at least a week after the Heintzelman, changed courses when only three days out of its New York destination. The MB Stewart picked up 150 men at random from the Heintzelman. Why only 150? I'll never know, but I returned to New York on the MB Stewart. I have no idea how and when the 1,350 servicemen still aboard the

Heintzelman returned to the U.S. but I'll never forget the jealous looks on their faces as we shoved off.

About six months later I heard the entire episode of the Heintzelman was written into the Congressional Record. Allegedly, the three individuals I described earlier were court martialed and convicted on major felony charges.

For the past year, I've made every effort possible to verify my personal accounting of the activities aboard the General Stuart Heintzelman during the first three weeks of January 1947. I have evidence that I was aboard this ship during this period. In addition, I have a photograph of the Stuart Heintzelman at anchor in the harbor of Ponta Delgada in the Azores Islands.

I have examined records of virtually every voyage the ship made from its original launching on April 21, 1945 to its deactivation on June 24, 1954, and its final berth with the National Defense Fleet in Beaumont, Texas.

I have researched the National Archives, the Department of the U.S. Army Center of Military History, and the Army and Navy Transport Service. I have information on the many citations and campaign ribbons that the General Stuart Heintzelman and its crews were awarded. I have names of some of the officers who commanded the ship during its history.

Some thousands of personnel, both military and civilian, called the General Stuart Heintzelman, "The Ship of Hope." I have labeled it "The Ship of Shame." Somewhere something's been hidden.

I personally saw food riots and race riots. Allegedly provisions for feeding the troops were sold on the black market. And I can't forget the assault by 750 troop members when they got shore leave on Ponta Delgada. Why was all this kept quiet? Is there a conspiracy of silence?

In addition to my own research and my attempts to obtain the ship's log for this specific period, Congresswoman Ellen Tauscher and her cooperative staff have also been unable to find (or get access to) this vital document. It has simply disappeared—or never existed.

Actually, the three weeks I spent on the General Stuart Heintzelman along with the five days on the General M.B. Stewart which finally brought me home, was the climax of my military service. But over 60 years later while researching this project, many meaningful and fascinating memories came flooding back to me. I believe that the Heintzelman experience helped trigger my reason for recalling and then researching so many elements of this book.

Epilogue

Having passed my 80th birthday, I can't help looking back at my earlier days and concluding that I have lived a rewarding life.

On reflection, the two years I spent in military service were one of the most meaningful periods in my life. I went from an 18-year-old college student, to a responsible adult.

I remember vividly the well-meaning friends and family who before I entered military service admonished me with, "Never volunteer for anything!" I broke that concept quickly by volunteering for everything. This choice served me well.

From my first experience of cruel anti-Semitism to observing the horror of the Holocaust, I saw human nature at its worst and the results of compassion and human kindness at its best.

The values learned during this period have served as a beacon of enlightenment for my entire life. Responsibility, accountability, and communication with others were an essential part of this learning process. Without question, these characteristics were developed during my military service.

Photos

Lou

With sister, Harriet, Camp Robinson,
1945

With dad, Harry, Camp Robinson, AR. 1945

With Marv as ROTC cadets, 1941

With Marv Spira, New York, 2004

Vera and Bill Armstrong today

With Ulli and John Carley, Carmel, California, 2004

Jean and Bob Tharratt, today

With Bob Tharratt, Memorial Day, 2006

With Ray Slominski, Walnut Creek, California, 2005

John Bednarezyk

Lou's Jeep, summer, 1946